THE QUEEN

101 Reasons to Celebrate Her Majesty

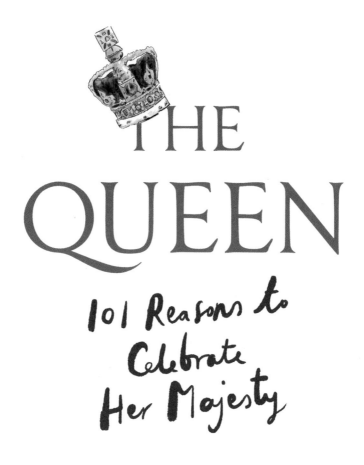

THE QUEEN

101 Reasons to
Celebrate
Her Majesty

E. Dunne & H. Sutcliffe

First published as *101 Reasons Why We Love the Queen*
in 2020 by Short Books Ltd
an imprint of Octopus Publishing Group Ltd
Carmelite House, 50 Victoria Embankment
London, EC4Y 0DZ
www.octopusbooks.co.uk
www.shortbooks.co.uk

An Hachette UK Company
www.hachette.co.uk

This new edition published in 2022

10 9 8 7 6 5 4 3 2 1

A CIP catalogue record for this book is
available from the British Library.

ISBN: 978-1-78072-548-2

Cover and page layouts by Two Associates
Illustrations by Evie Dunne

Printed in Italy by Printer Trento S.r.l.

For Her Majesty

INTRODUCTION

I N PERIODS OF UNCERTAINTY, it is natural for us to look for beacons of stability and strength. Her Majesty is surely *the* beacon of beacons. She has been the calm and composed face of our nation (and our postage stamps) for a very long time. What is it about this nonagenarian, 5-foot-4-inch woman, in her bright suits and pearls, that inspires such admiration and respect? This little book attempts to address that big question.

The Queen has been a rare constant in a world of exponential change. Her Majesty's reign has seen 14 British prime ministers come and go, she has outlived five popes and seen one retire. For 70 years, she has been the nation's figurehead;

from the swinging sixties and the moon landings to the advent of the computer and WhatsApp…. She has seen it all.

The role of a monarch is not what it once was. Henry VIII and his many wives, Charles I and his 'royal prerogative', Charles II with his riotous parties… executions aside, they all had quite a good time of it. These days, the monarchy retains the aura of sovereignty but has lost much of its power. To some extent, the monarchy has to earn its right to stay, and in an age when republicanism is in the ascendancy, it says everything about the current Queen that she is so widely adored.

Every summer, the Queen hosts three garden parties at Buckingham Palace – 10,000 guests attending each one. She carries out countless visits to schools, hospitals, factories and unveilings around the country, attends endless meetings, fields endless questions, all the while seemingly remaining a paragon of decorum and calm. An expert in the art of small talk, she has a way of making everyone – from heads of state to subjects from around the world – feel at ease. 'It's rather nice to feel that one is a sort of sponge, and everybody can come and tell one things,' she has said of her weekly meetings with prime ministers over the years.

Most of us love nothing more than to off-load about the weather, or better still, give detailed descriptions of motorway journeys or commuting patterns to anyone who will listen. Always one to instinctively read the mood of her people, the Queen has a ready stock of useful icebreakers. 'Have you come far?' is said to be one of her favourites, a fail-safe way of drawing out lengthy travel anecdotes as well as woeful tales of weather disruptions. On one such occasion, the answer to this question prompted a moving and memorable encounter. Dr David Nott has described how, soon after returning from his work as a war surgeon in Syria, he was invited to a lunch at Buckingham Palace. With familiar politeness, the Queen asked him where he had come from.

'Aleppo', he replied. As memories of the terrible suffering he had witnessed there came flooding back to him, Dr Nott's 'bottom lip started to go', and he was unable to speak. Sensing that he was traumatised and lost for words, the Queen took some biscuits out of a box in front of her. 'These are for the dogs'. For the rest of the lunch, the two of them fed and petted the corgis under the table. 'There,' said the Queen. 'That's so much better than talking, isn't it?'

Her Majesty seems to have mastered the Herculean challenge of being all things to everyone. An imposing figurehead for a nation and the Commonwealth, decked out in diamonds and regalia, she is also just as content when wearing wellies and a raincoat, walking her dogs or spending time with her grandchildren and great-grandchildren. But perhaps the place she is most at home is among her horses. The Queen's first pony, Peggy, was given to her as a fourth birthday present from her grandfather George V, and her love and great knowledge of all things equestrian has been lifelong. Anyone who has watched footage of her at the Epsom Derby in 1991 can see the transformation that occurs when the Queen visits a race course. We see Her Majesty running from the Royal Box, balancing her glasses on her forehead to watch through a pair of binoculars, as the horse she has drawn from the royal sweepstake wins the race. As her cousin, Margaret Rhodes, puts it, 'She has had to sacrifice within herself an awful lot of emotions… in those sort of moments, she can let rip with real excitement.'

But these moments are rare, and it is her self-discipline and self-awareness which make her such a remarkable queen. Despite living under constant scrutiny, she never appears to put a toe out of line. Over the course of her reign, she has handled situations of explosive importance, both global and personal, with wisdom and tact. As she said in 2015, when she became the world's longest reigning monarch, 'A long life can pass by many milestones, and mine is no exception.' But of course, her life has been exceptional, and the milestones in it have been unlike anything most of us will experience. It is this ability to remind us of a common humanity and history that makes her so uniquely important.

THE
QUEEN

*101 Reasons to
Celebrate
Her Majesty*

She is the only person who can attract a
Glastonbury-sized crowd
without singing a single note.

The Queen has owned more than 30 corgis.
Her first corgi, Susan, was given to her by King
George VI on her 18th birthday. On her death, the
beloved Susan was buried at Sandringham with a
headstone personally designed by the Queen.

For breakfast, the Queen likes a choice of
cornflakes or porridge oats, which she keeps in
Tupperware containers.

She gave her first public broadcast aged 14
with her sister Princess Margaret. It was addressed
to the children of the Commonwealth to
boost morale during the Second World War.

The Queen likes to wake up to the sound of
bagpipes.

She preserves traditions – and even revives old ones.
From 1630 the monarch used to give the
Poet Laureate a 'butt of sack', now known as
sherry. The tradition lapsed in 1800. Her Majesty
reinstated it – but with 720 bottles.

She is thrifty and resourceful.

When she married Prince Philip in 1947, rationing was still in place and she paid for her wedding dress by saving up ration coupons.

She has worn the same style of patent black,
low-heeled court shoe handmade by
Anello & Davide for the last fifty years.
She keeps ten pairs on rotation at a time, with
two new pairs made every year for her.

She has been the inspiration for the mug
and china collections of people around the world.

She's a huge party thrower –
hosting 30,000 people
every year at her garden parties.

She has an epic stamp collection, inherited from
George V, that she continues to add to. It is so
massive it is said to fill 300 albums and
200 boxes – all kept securely in a vault at
St James's Palace.

Her favourite flower

is the

humble primrose.

She had a brief spell as an actress putting on Christmas pantomimes with Princess Margaret during the war. In 2013, Her Majesty was awarded an honorary BAFTA – not for her panto performances, but for her support of British film and television.

She is passionate about horse racing.

She drives a Land Rover in a
silk headscarf,

and even chauffeured a Saudi prince on a tour
of Balmoral once – much to his surprise,
particularly as women in Saudi Arabia were
not permitted to drive at the time.

Her Majesty's lunch aperitif is a cocktail of
Dubonnet with a slug of gin on the rocks.
Dubonnet is a sweet fortified wine blended with
spices and herbs invented by a French chemist.

Very fortifying.

She is a trained mechanic, from her time
in the Auxiliary Territorial Service during the
Second World War.

She has not one but TWO birthdays.

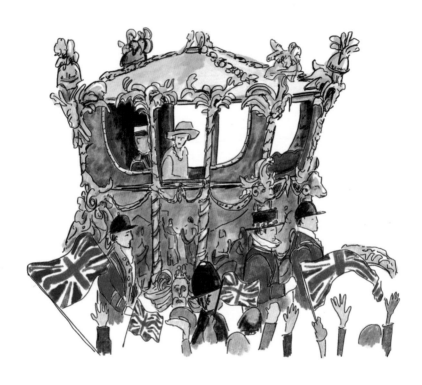

She is always surrounded by the most fantastic
pomp and splendour for ceremonial events.

♔

20

Her corgis have wonderful names.

As do her spaniels, Bisto, Oxo, Spick, Span…

Her silk head scarves are a staple
accessory in her off-duty wardrobe, providing a
regal elegance to her casual attire.

Her bodyguards, the 'Yeomen of the Guard' wear
uniforms that haven't changed since the day the
guards were formed in 1485. They are the oldest
British military corps still in existence.

23

She is the only person who can drag people away
from their roast turkeys on Christmas day.

She has recorded a Christmas address to the nation
every year since 1952 – except in 1969, when
a special documentary film was made on the Royal
Family and the Queen issued a written
Christmas message instead.

To get herself to sleep at night, when she was
little, she would imagine riding her horses around
Windsor Great Park. She told her governess it was to
exercise her horses.

She owns more than 200 handbags, all made
by Launer. She favours a slightly longer handle
so it doesn't get caught up in her clothes when
she is greeting people.

She receives around 300 letters every day...

... and reads almost all of them.

She has a superhuman ability

to keep on

waving.

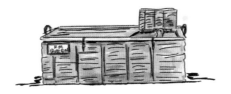

The Queen has 200 racing pigeons which she keeps
at Sandringham. The sport has been a royal hobby
since 1886, when King Leopold II of Belgium gave
some racing pigeons to the Royal Family.

She has an umbrella to match every outfit.

Come rain or shine, Her Majesty is a

one colour palette lady.

Her Majesty enjoys and is very good at

washing up,

which she does after her annual barbecue

parties at Balmoral.

She lives in Buckingham Palace.

She has a sweet tooth, with a particular
penchant for chocolate.

She was the first British monarch
to visit the Republic of Ireland.

Her hairstyle over the years has been as
consistent and steadfast as her leadership.

She can ride side saddle, and did so in the procession for the Trooping of the Colour until 1987 (since then she has attended in a carriage).

She knows how to work a
supermarket self-checkout.

She is the patron of over 600 charities, and has done
more for charity than any other monarch in history –
raising a total of around £1.4 billion.

Her Majesty is the epitome of
trustworthiness and stability.

She is a unifying force wherever she goes.

Her dogs travel everywhere with her.
She even took her first corgi, Susan,
on her honeymoon.

She has been given a menagerie of animals
from all over the world, including a sloth, two black
jaguars, a crocodile and an elephant, all of which
she has gifted to London Zoo.

She has made over 250 official overseas
trips during her reign, making her the most widely
travelled British monarch in history.

She is the master of pithy remarks.

The Queen has a gold Blue Peter badge – the programme's highest honour – awarded in 2002 to celebrate her 50 years on the throne.

46

The queen loves jigsaw puzzles and usually
keeps a giant set waiting to be finished in each of her
palaces. Every year she pays a subscription to
borrow complicated puzzles from the
British Jigsaw Puzzle Library.

She loves musicals.

Oklahoma! is one of her favourites.

She is always delighted when her horse wins a race.
In 2013, she wept tears of joy when she became
the first reigning monarch to win the Gold Cup
in the 207-year history of the race. And of course, her
suit matched the jockey's colours.

... And following tradition, all the men doff their
top hats when the Queen's horse wins.

She has a brooch for every occasion.

She has simple tastes. According to a previous royal
butler, the Queen enjoys cucumber sandwiches on
white bread, crusts off naturally.

People stand up straighter when they are near her –
very good for one's posture.

She can end a meeting just by
ringing a bell.

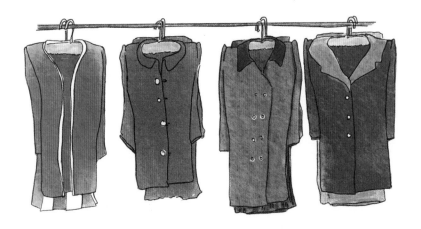

The Queen has an eminently practical wardrobe
of matching rainbow suits, to ensure that she
can always be spotted in a crowd.

She plants trees.

55

Along with 72 other world leaders, she sent a message to celebrate the moon landings, which was taken by Neil Armstrong and Buzz Aldrin on the historic Apollo 11 mission.

She does her own makeup
(except for one special occasion –
the Christmas speech).

She is not a celebrity.

She has a great sense of humour, allowing herself
to be turned into a Bond Girl for London's 2012
Olympic opening ceremony.

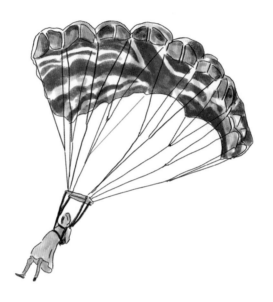

She even parachuted from a helicopter

as part of the performance.

It was definitely her!

She has a fantastic hat collection – no frothy fascinators for Her Majesty. The Queen wears proper hats.

♔

61

She cleverly puts small lead curtain weights
in her hemlines to prevent any mishaps
in windy weather.

She is very economical. She always makes sure
the lights are turned off when leaving a room.

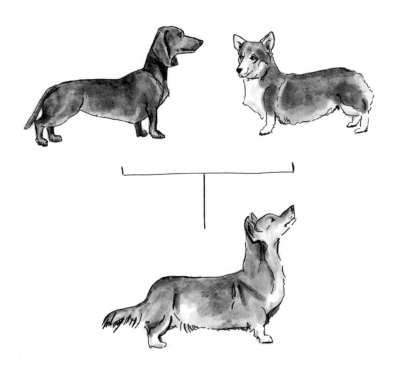

She has established an entirely new dog breed –
the dorgi, a cross between a corgi
and a dachshund.

She is a music lover, attending concerts of all
kinds, supporting musical organisations and founding
The Queen's Medal for Music, awarded to those
who have had a major influence on the
musical life of the nation.

She loves Scottish dancing. Each year during
her stay at Balmoral Castle, the Queen gives dances
known as Gillies' Balls, for her neighbours, staff
and members of the local community.

She **still rides** her horse regularly
– and always in a headscarf.

She is above politics.

She sends a personalised birthday message
to centenarians – the best incentive
to live to 100.

She credits her good health and longevity
to drinking one glass of champagne every day.

She is not afraid to be
bold with lipstick.

She stepped up when her father died
and just got on with it, despite being only 25
when she acceded the throne.

She loves the sweet-smelling flower, Lily of the

Valley, which was in both her wedding and

coronation bouquets. On being told that the flower

was once used as poison, Her Majesty said,

'I've been given two bunches this week.

Perhaps they want me dead.'

Her long marriage to Prince Philip – of 73 years –
was an inspiration to all couples. She said of him:
'He has, quite simply, been my strength and stay
all these years.'

She adores the British countryside.

She enjoys card games, particularly
Patience.

Her coronation gave rise to one of the nation's favourite dishes, Coronation Chicken, originally called Chicken Elizabeth.

Her wedding cake was

nine

foot

tall.

She owns many jewels but prefers to wear
the same sets of pearls, timeless and classic,
just like herself.

79

She has her own tartan. As the reigning monarch,
she is the sole owner of the 'Balmoral' tartan, designed
by Prince Albert in 1853. Even fellow members of the
Royal Family have to ask her permission to wear it.

She has kept a diary since she was a teenager,
recording her thoughts every night before bed.
She manages 15 minutes' writing before
she starts dozing off.

81

She knows when and how
to pick her battles.

CARAVAGGIO

She has the largest privately owned art collection in
the world, with paintings by most of Western art's
greatest figures, and has made much of it
accessible to the public by opening
the Queen's Gallery in 1962.

She has a herd of over 60 Highland Cattle,

including a prizewinning bull called

Ruaraidh 1st of Ubhaidh.

Two members of the Somerset and Avon Police force
have been officially named by the Queen –
the horses, 'Windsor' and 'Jubilee'
('Lovely Jubbly' for short).

She embraces change – from her televised coronation
to the royal Twitter account to Zoom calls
with care workers during lockdown.

A little picture of the Queen by Arnold Machin, as
seen on our postage stamps, is the world's most
reproduced artwork, way ahead of the Mona Lisa,
with more than 220 billion copies reproduced
in the 45 years since it was made.

The Queen has given out about 75,000 Christmas
puddings to staff, continuing the custom started by
her grandfather, King George V.

Even die-hard republicans have
been brought round to her.

She records her Christmas speech
in one take – what a professional.

She has sent more than 50,000 Christmas cards

in her lifetime – and counting.

The Queen enjoys reading detective fiction,
as her mother did. PD James and Dick Francis are
particular favourites – Dick Francis used to send
a first edition copy of his latest thriller
to the Queen Mother.

VANITY FAIR

She is a pin-up and an icon
for how to age gracefully.

She is able to weather storms,

both personal and political,

with quiet resilience and nerves of steel.

She is fastidious about keeping up to date with her
photo albums, all of which she does herself.

She is always dignified,

graceful and composed.

She holds four Guinness World Records:
she is the world's longest reigning queen,
the world's oldest reigning monarch,
the world's wealthiest queen,
and she appears on the money of more
sovereign countries than any other person.

She reminds us of our 20th century history.

98

Her birthday **fly-pasts** are a treat for all.

She is brilliant at small talk.

She is not only monarch,
but also mother of four, grandmother of eight and
great-grandmother of twelve.

That smile.